D1369637

JOHN LEE HOOKER

Master of Boogie and Blues

By Therese Shea

Gareth Stevens
Publishing

Please visit our Web site www.garethstevens.com. For a free color catalog of all our high-quality books, call toll free 1-800-542-2595 or fax 1-877-542-2596.

Library of Congress Cataloging-in-Publication Data

Shea, Therese.
John Lee Hooker : master of boogie and blues / Therese Shea.
    p. cm. — (Inspiring lives)
Includes index.
ISBN 978-1-4339-3626-5 (pbk.)
ISBN 978-1-4339-3627-2 (6-pack)
ISBN 978-1-4339-3625-8 (library binding)
1. Hooker, John Lee—Juvenile literature. 2. Blues musicians—United States—Biography—Juvenile literature. I. Title.
ML3930.H67S54 2010
781.643092—dc22
[B]

2009037272

Published in 2010 by Gareth Stevens Publishing
111 East 14th Street, Suite 349
New York, NY 10003

Designer: Michael J. Flynn
Editor: Therese Shea

Photo credits: Cover (John Lee Hooker), pp. 1 (John Lee Hooker), 23 © Paul Natkin/WireImage/Getty Images; cover (stage), p. 1 (background) Shutterstock.com; p. 5 © Tom Copi/Michael Ochs Archives/Getty Images; pp. 7, 13, 17 © Michael Ochs Archives/Getty Images; p. 9 © Gilles Petard/Redferns/Getty Images; p. 11 © Val Wilmer/Redferns/Getty Images; p. 15 © Elliott Landy/Redferns/Getty Images; p. 19 © Richard E. Aaron/Redferns/Getty Images; p. 21 © Jan Persson/Redferns/Getty Images; pp. 25, 27 © Ebet Roberts/Redferns/Getty Images; p. 29 © John Chiasson/Getty Images.

Printed in the United States of America

CPSIA compliance information: Batch #CW10GS: For further information contact Gareth Stevens, New York, New York at 1-800-542-2595.

Contents

A Music Man

John Lee Hooker was a guitar player. He was a singer, too. He played and sang the blues and boogie music.

John's Family

John was born in 1917 near Clarksdale, Mississippi. His family worked on a farm. They were very poor.

Clarksdale

Jackson
★

MISSISSIPPI

John's stepfather taught him to play the guitar. He taught John about the blues.

Moving Away

John left his home to find a job. He moved to Detroit in 1943. He worked in a factory.

John played music for his friends after work. He played the blues. He played boogie music, too.

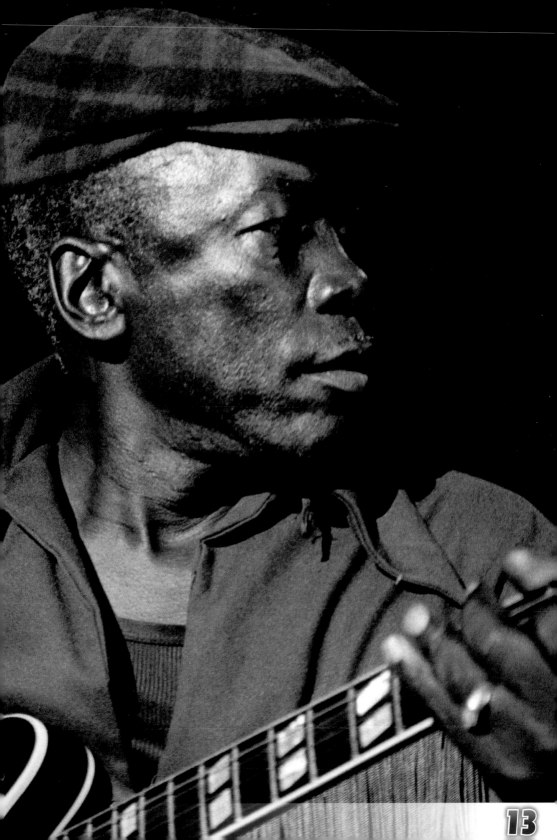

Making Hits

People liked John's music. A company asked John to make a record in 1948.

John's first record was "Boogie Chillen."

It played in jukeboxes all over the

United States.

John made more records. "Boom Boom" and "I'm in the Mood" were two more hits.

Becoming Famous

John played alone at first. Later, he played with other people.

John continued to play blues in the 1970s and 1980s. He was even in a movie called *The Blues Brothers*!

Honoring John

John won four Grammys. Many famous people have played his songs to honor him.

Huey Lewis

Albert Collins

Bo Diddley

John got another honor in 1991. He became part of the Rock and Roll Hall of Fame.

John Lee Hooker died in 2001. He made many people love the blues and boogie music.

Timeline

1917 John Lee Hooker is born near Clarksdale, Mississippi.

1943 John moves to Detroit.

1948 John makes "Boogie Chillen," the first of many records.

1980 John appears in the movie *The Blues Brothers.*

1989 John wins his first Grammy.

1991 John becomes part of the Rock and Roll Hall of Fame.

2001 John dies.

For More Information

Books:

Kennedy, Timothy. *Midnight Son: A Tribute to John Lee Hooker.*
Tampa, FL: University of Tampa Press, 2006.

Koopmans, Andy. *The History of the Blues.* San Diego, CA:
Lucent Books, 2005.

Weissman, Dick. *Blues.* New York: Checkmark Books, 2006.

Web Sites:

John Lee Hooker (1917–2001)

www.johnleehooker.com

Rock and Roll Hall of Fame and Museum: John Lee Hooker

www.rockhall.com/inductee/john-lee-hooker

Glossary

blues: a kind of sad music

boogie: music that has a strong beat and is good for dancing

Grammy: an honor given each year for writing or playing music

jukebox: a machine that plays recorded music when you put in money

record: a round, flat object that stores and plays back sounds

Index